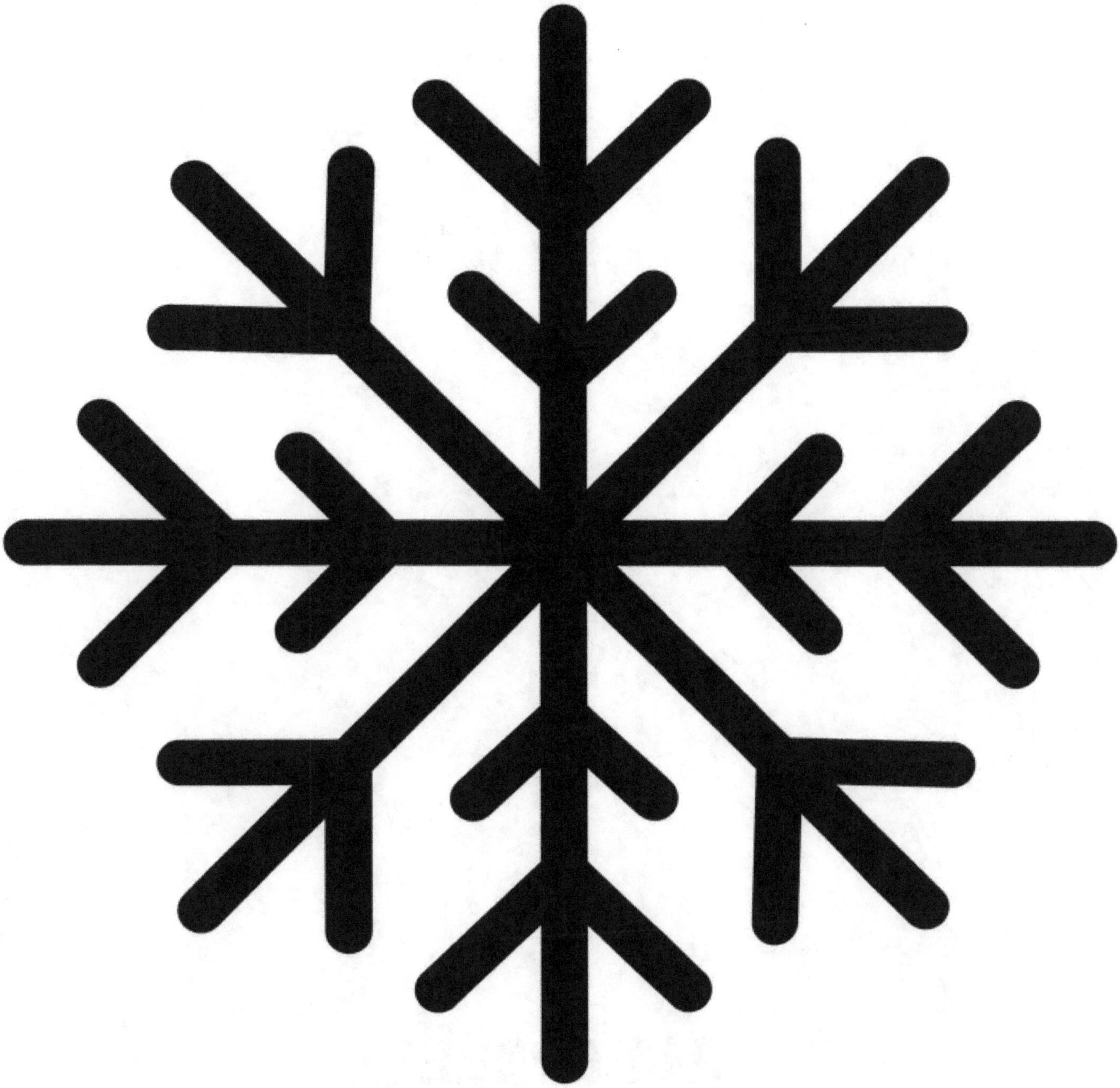

PAPERBLES

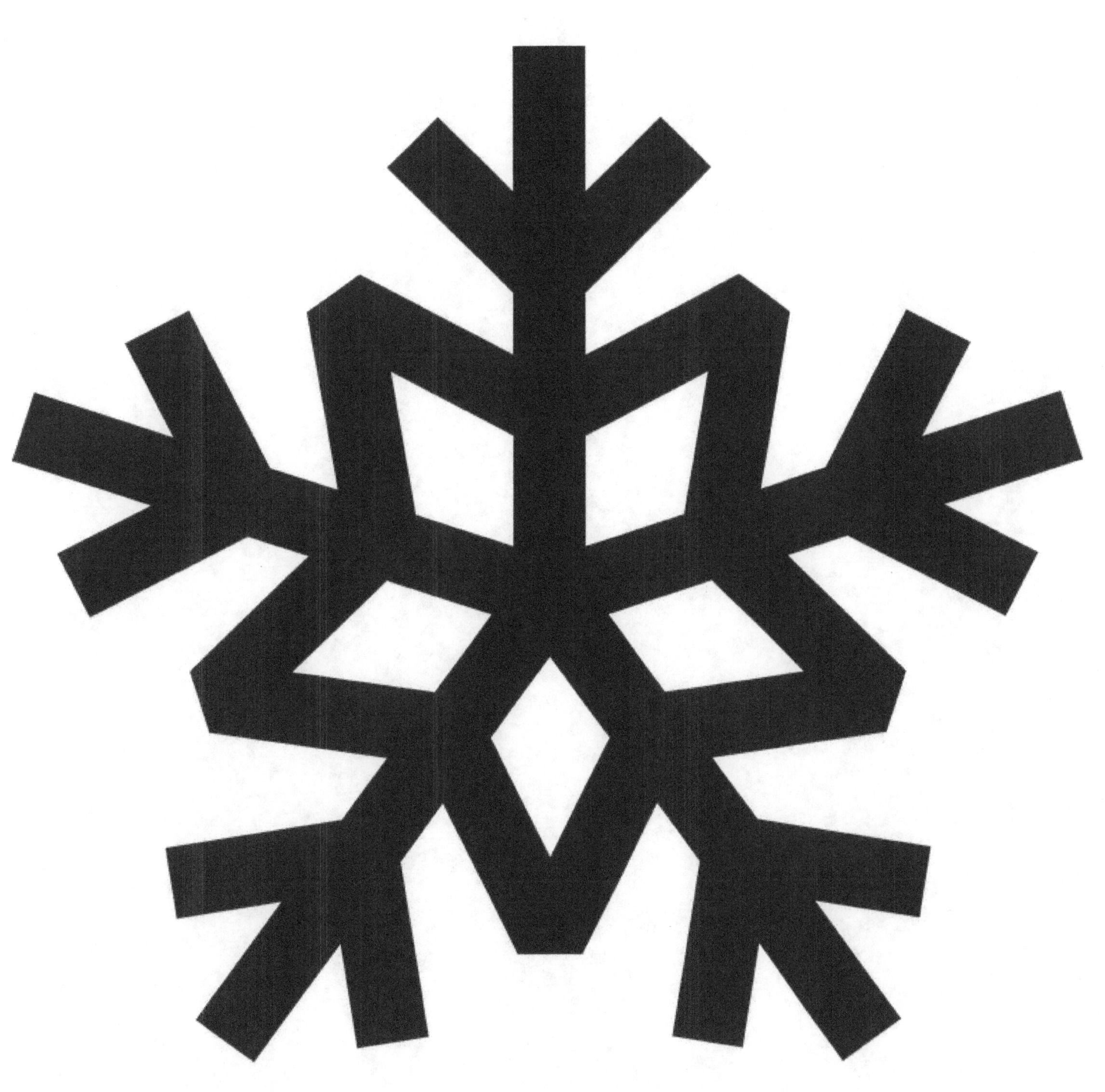

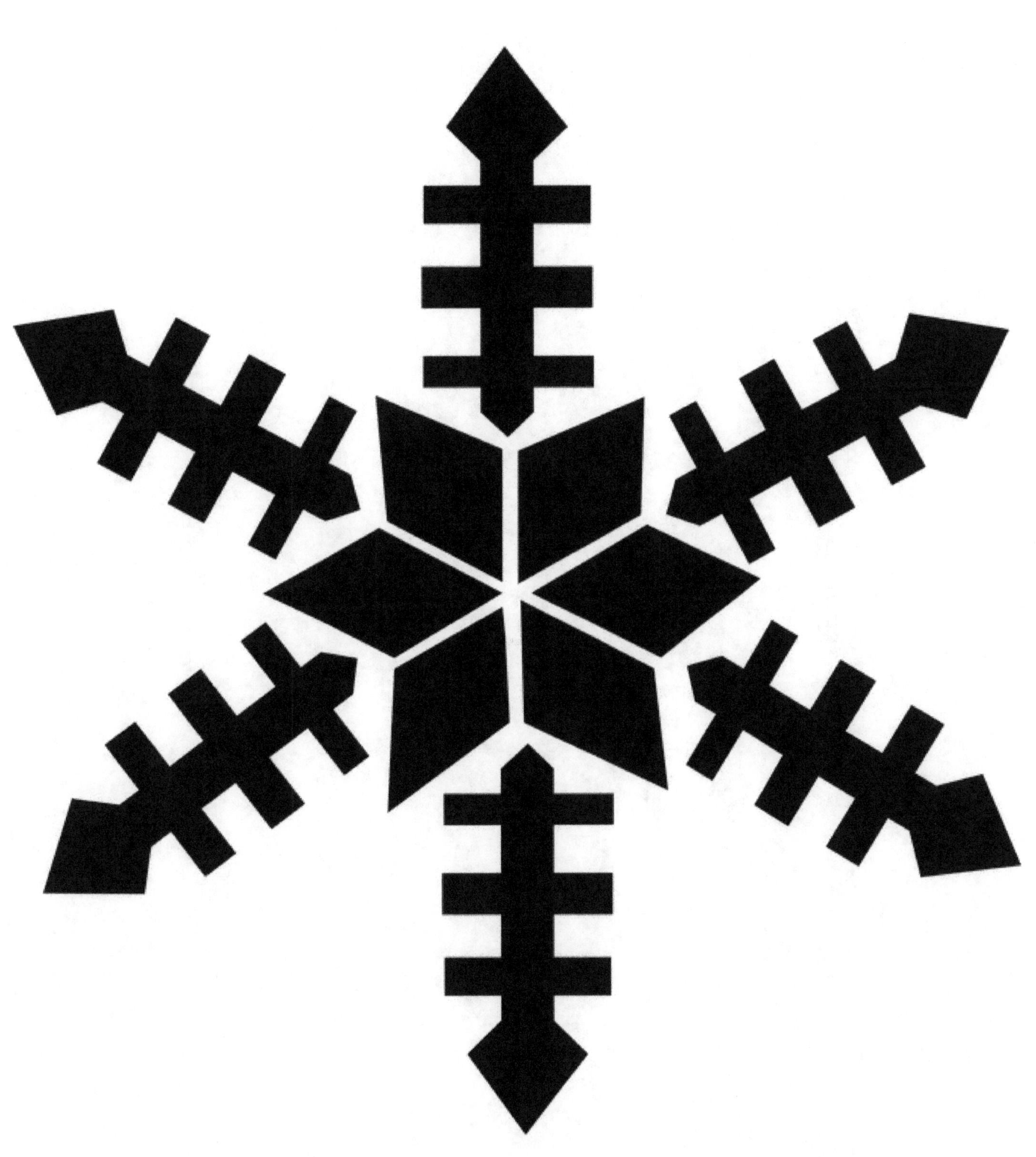

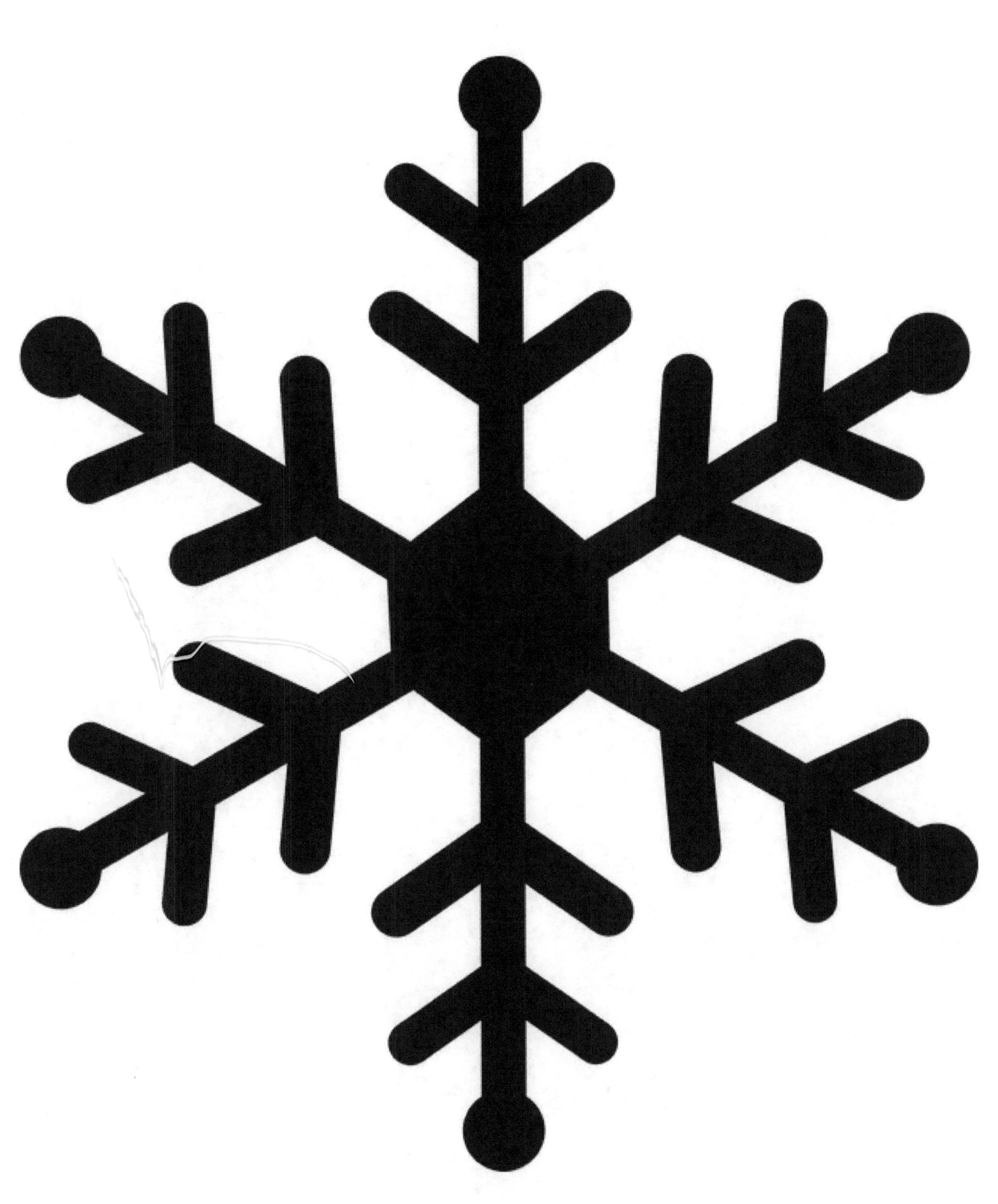

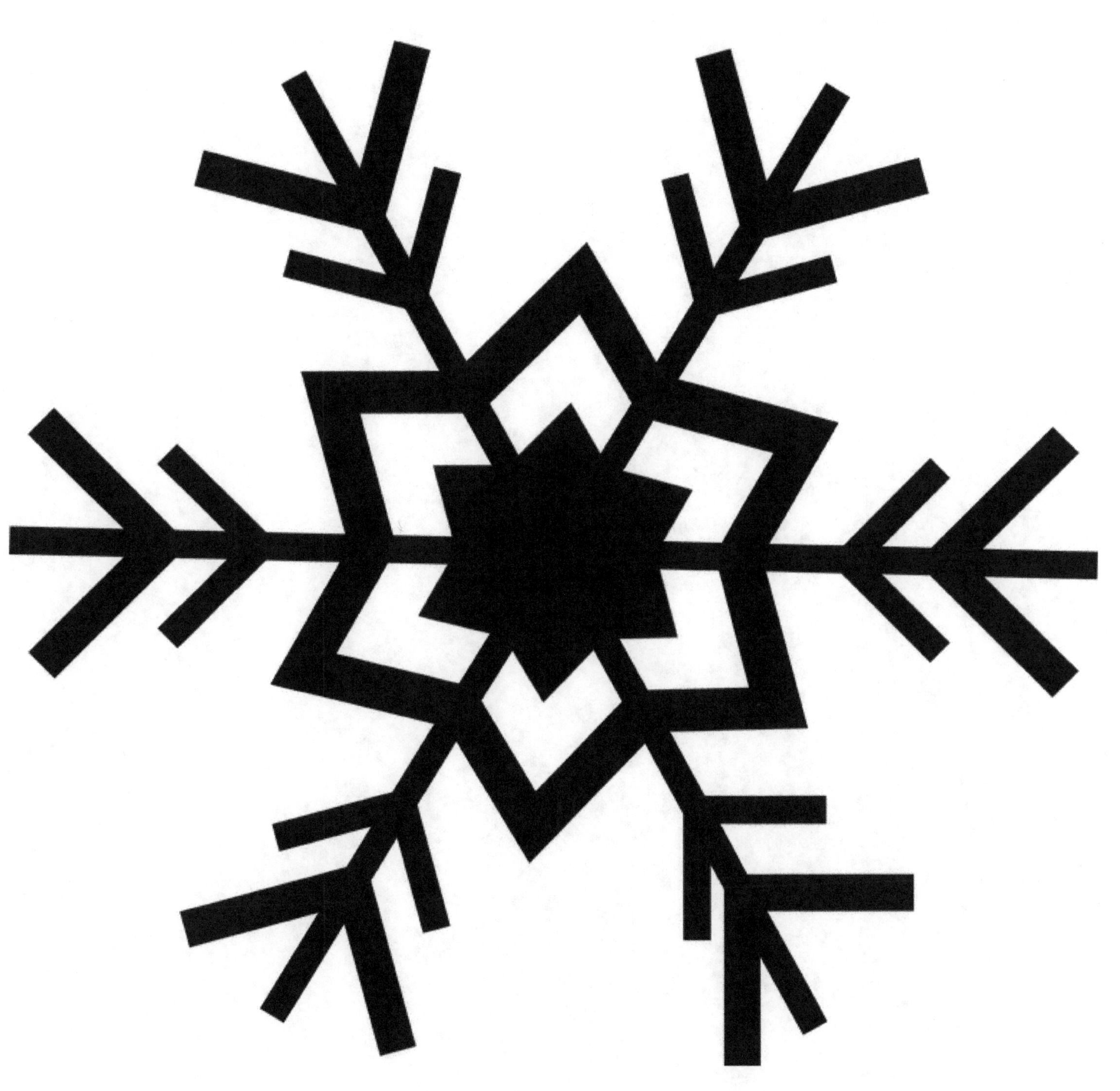

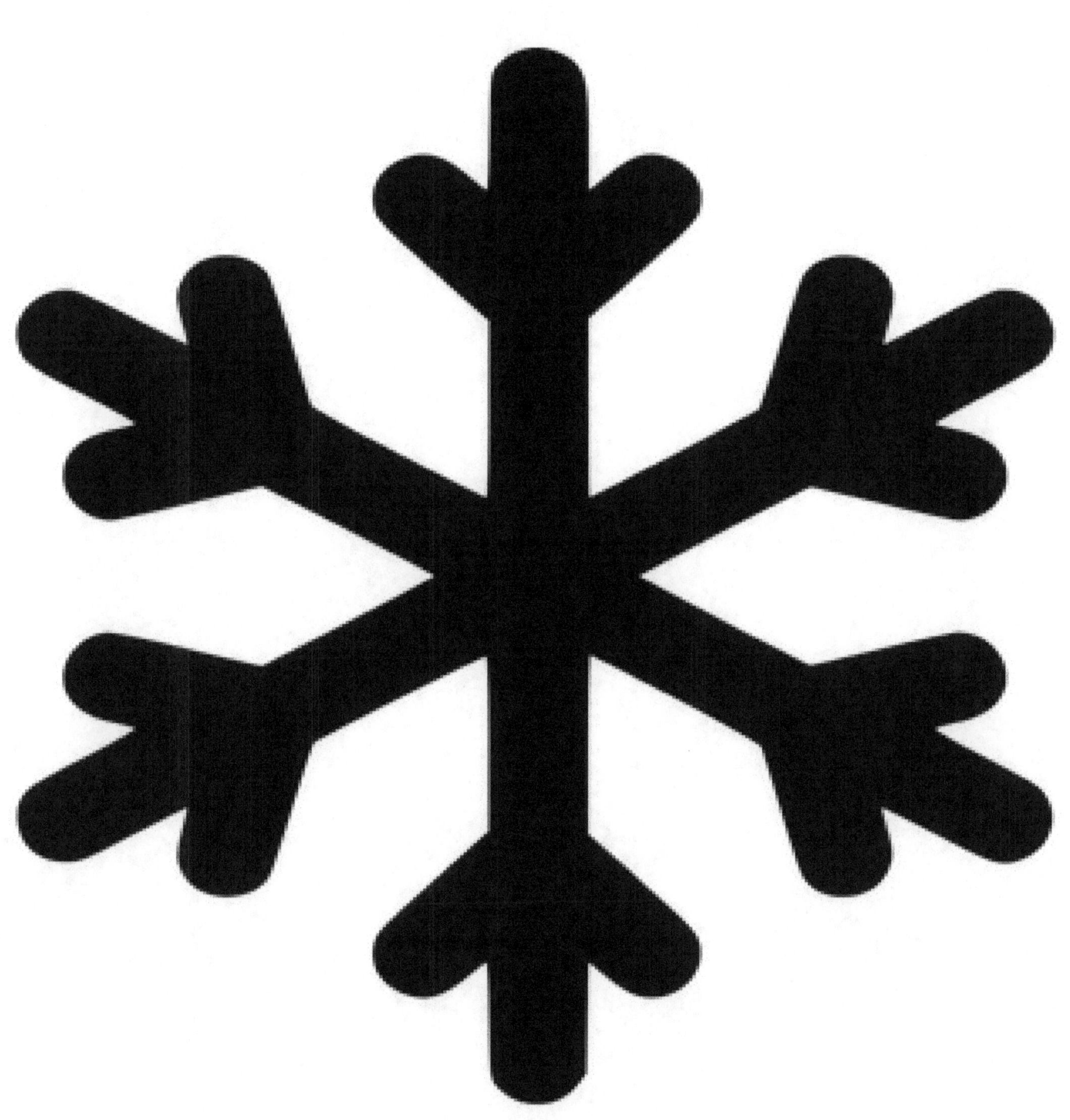

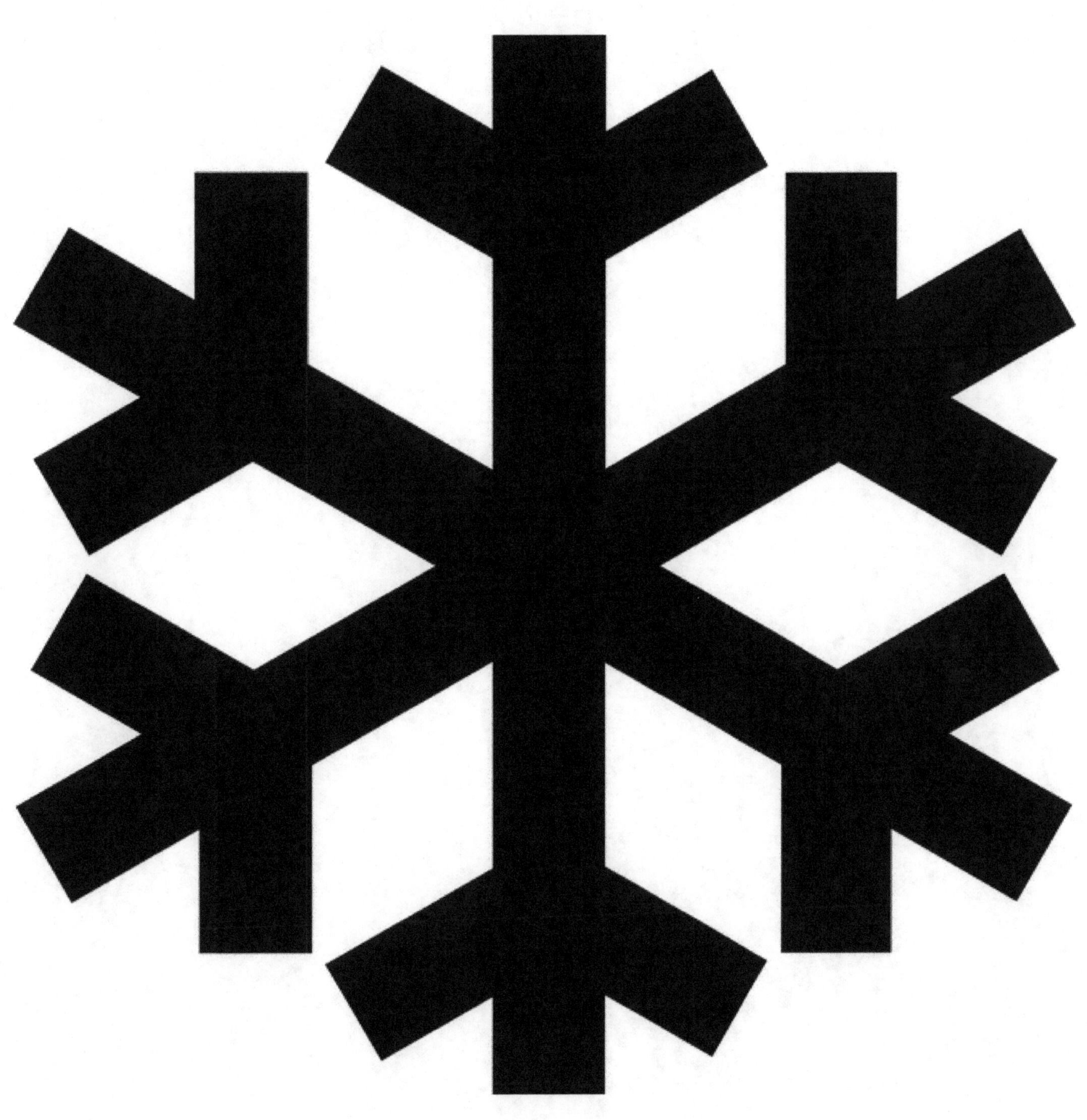

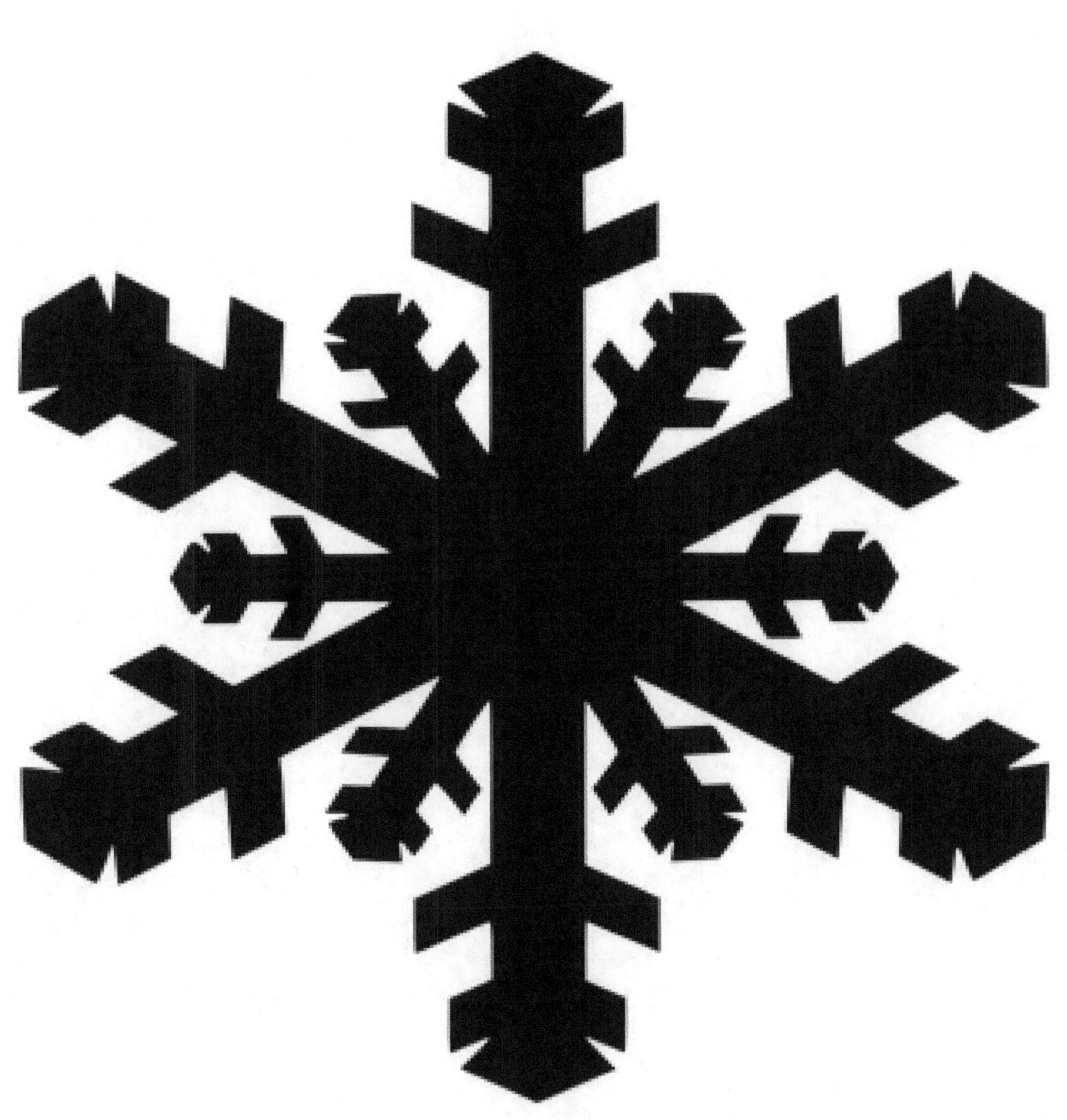

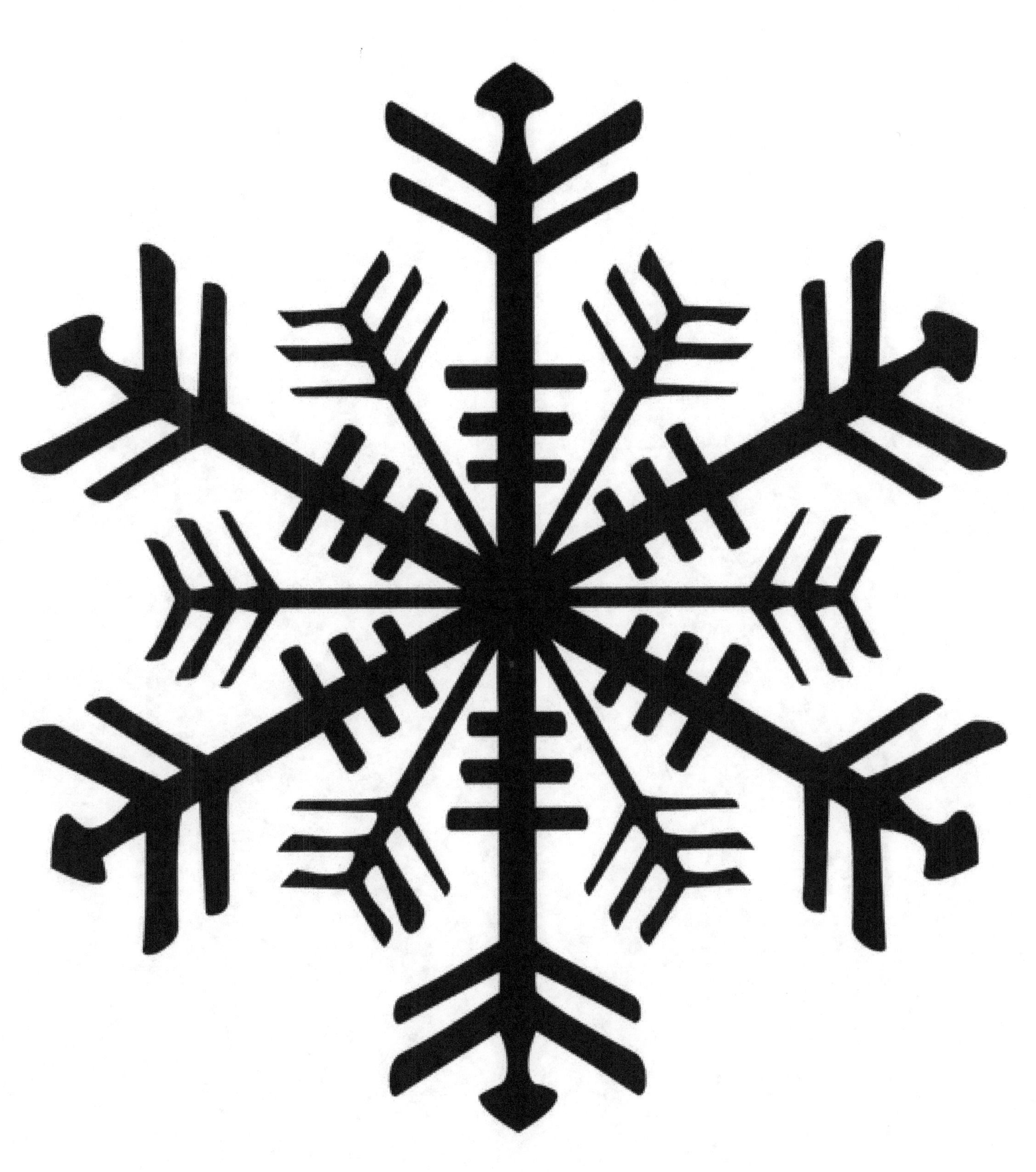

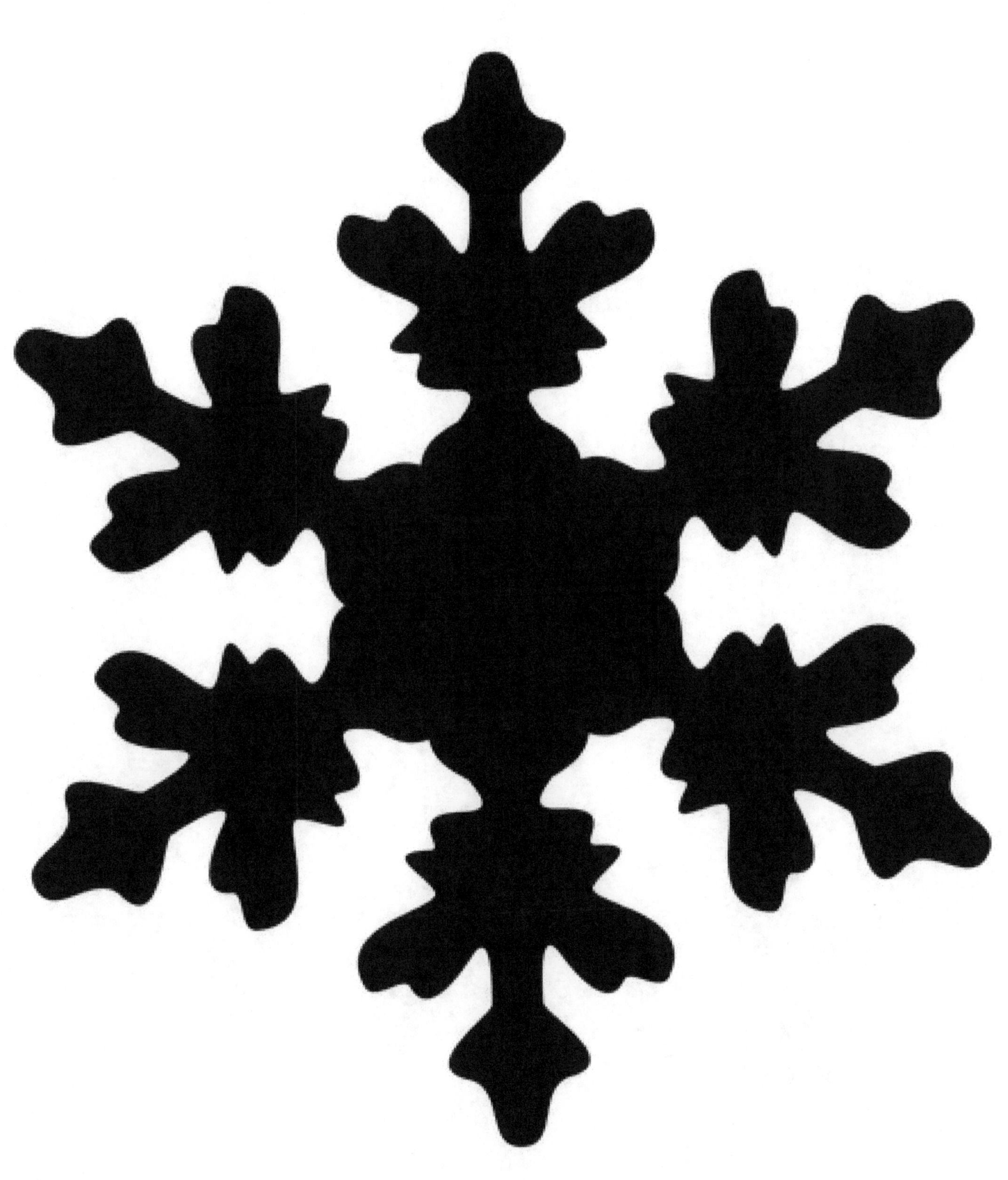

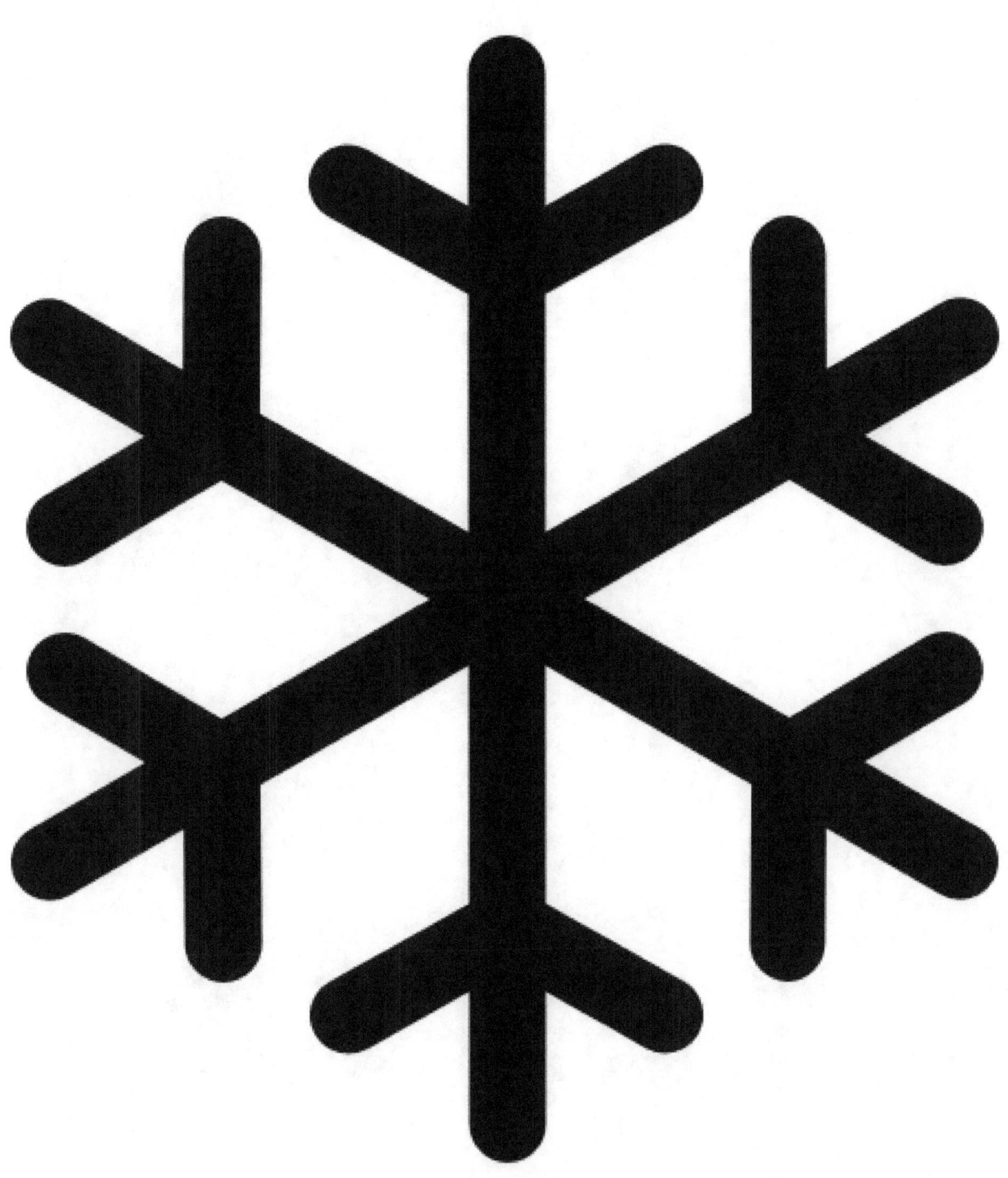

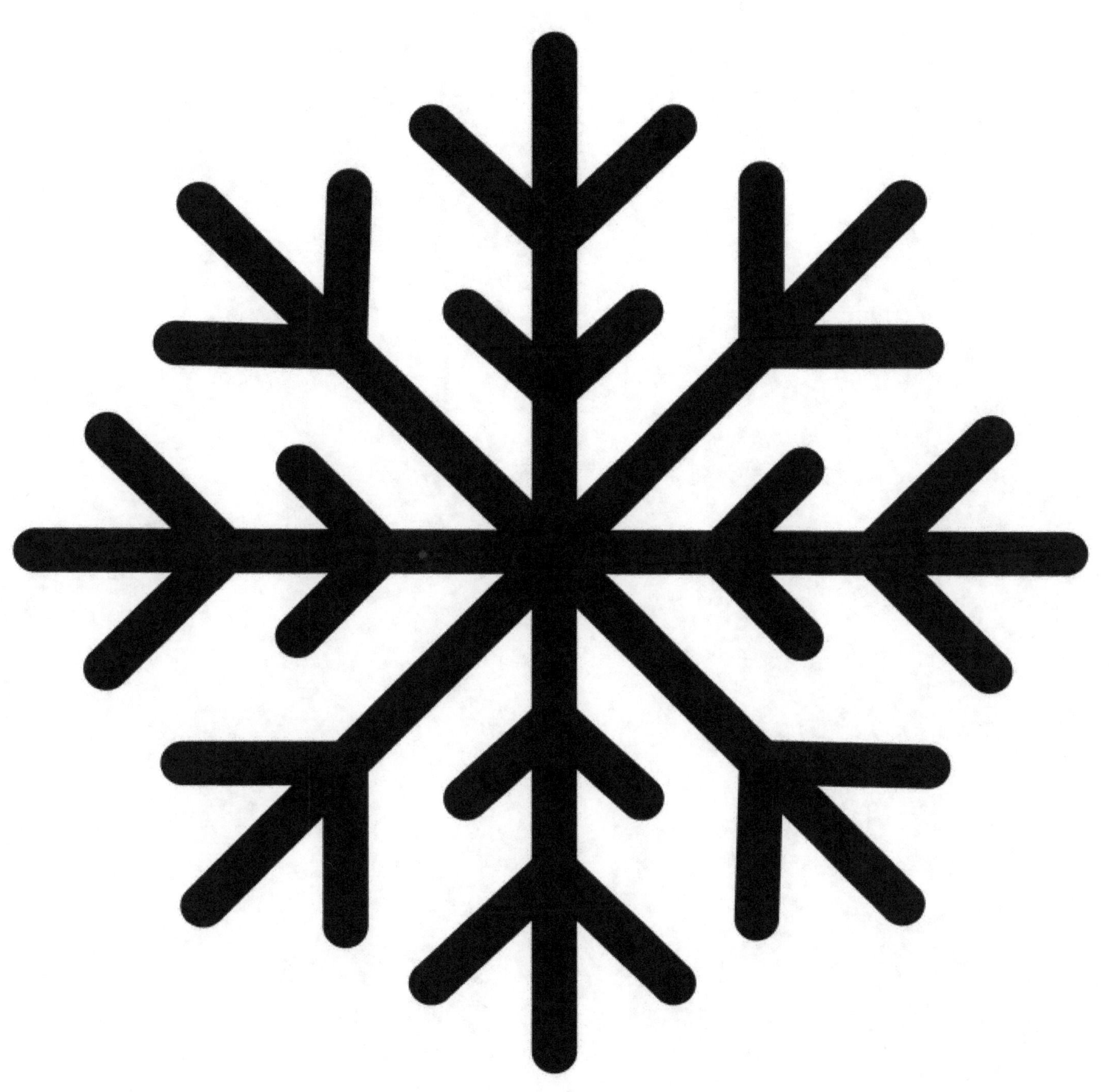

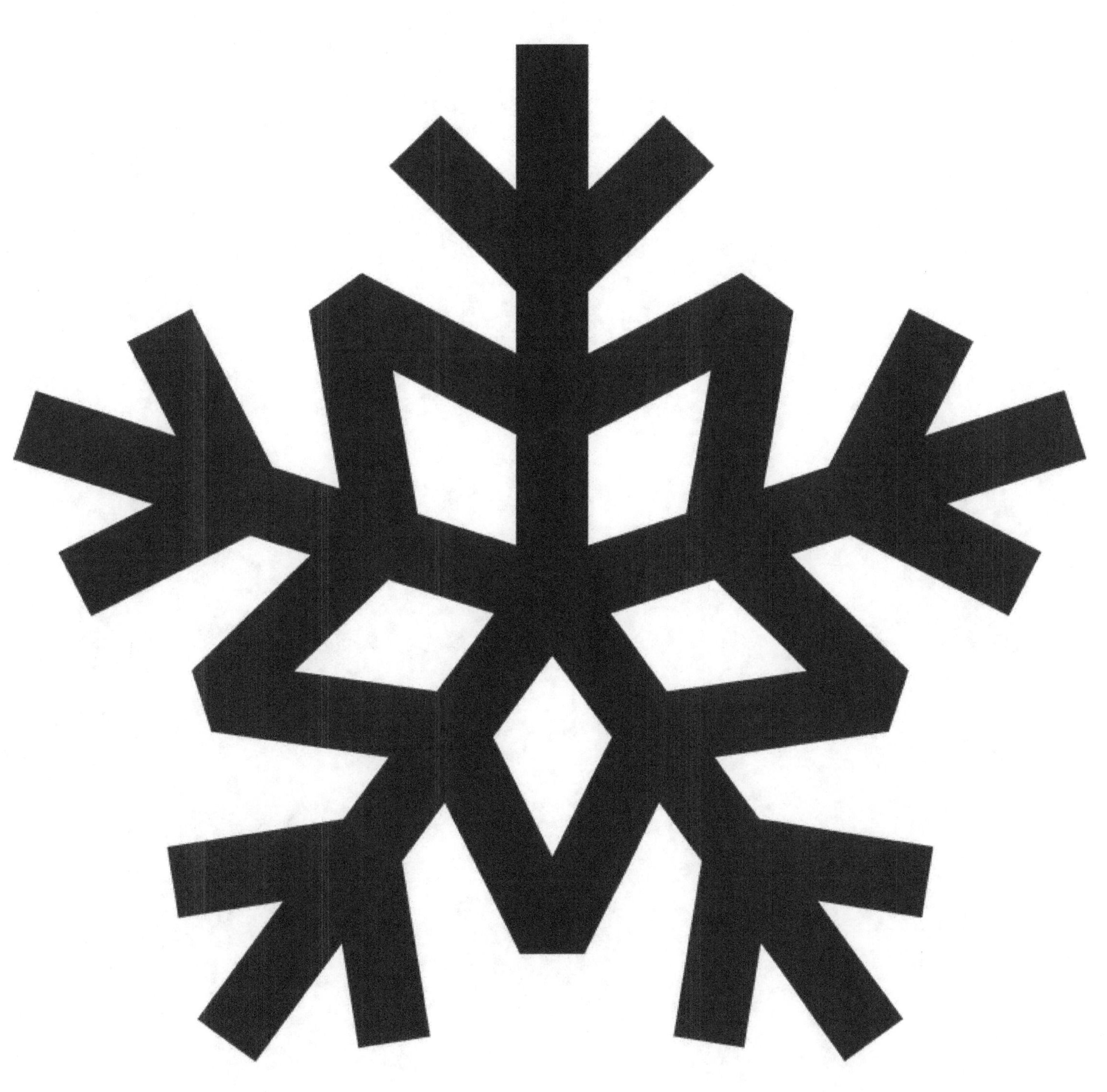

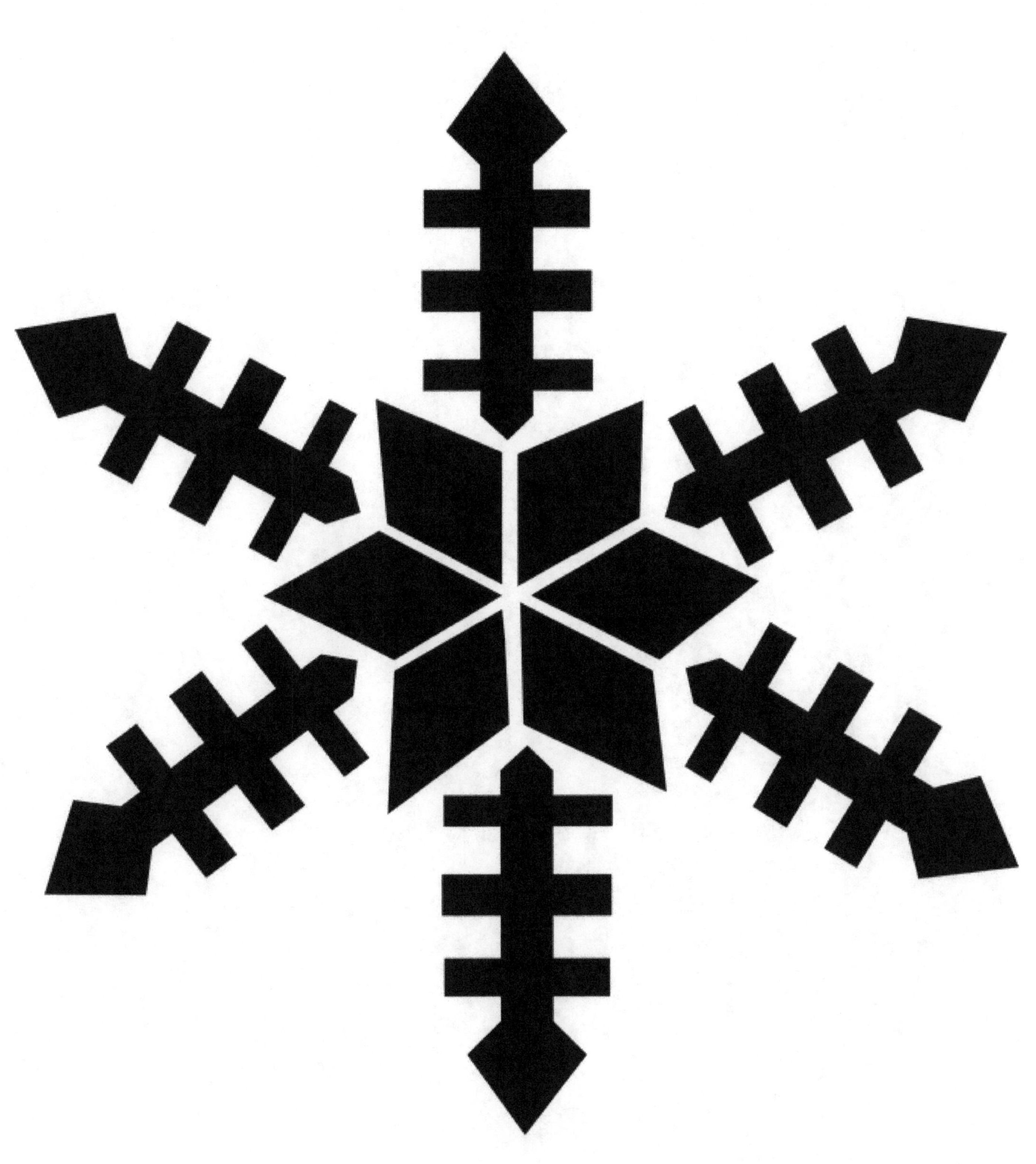

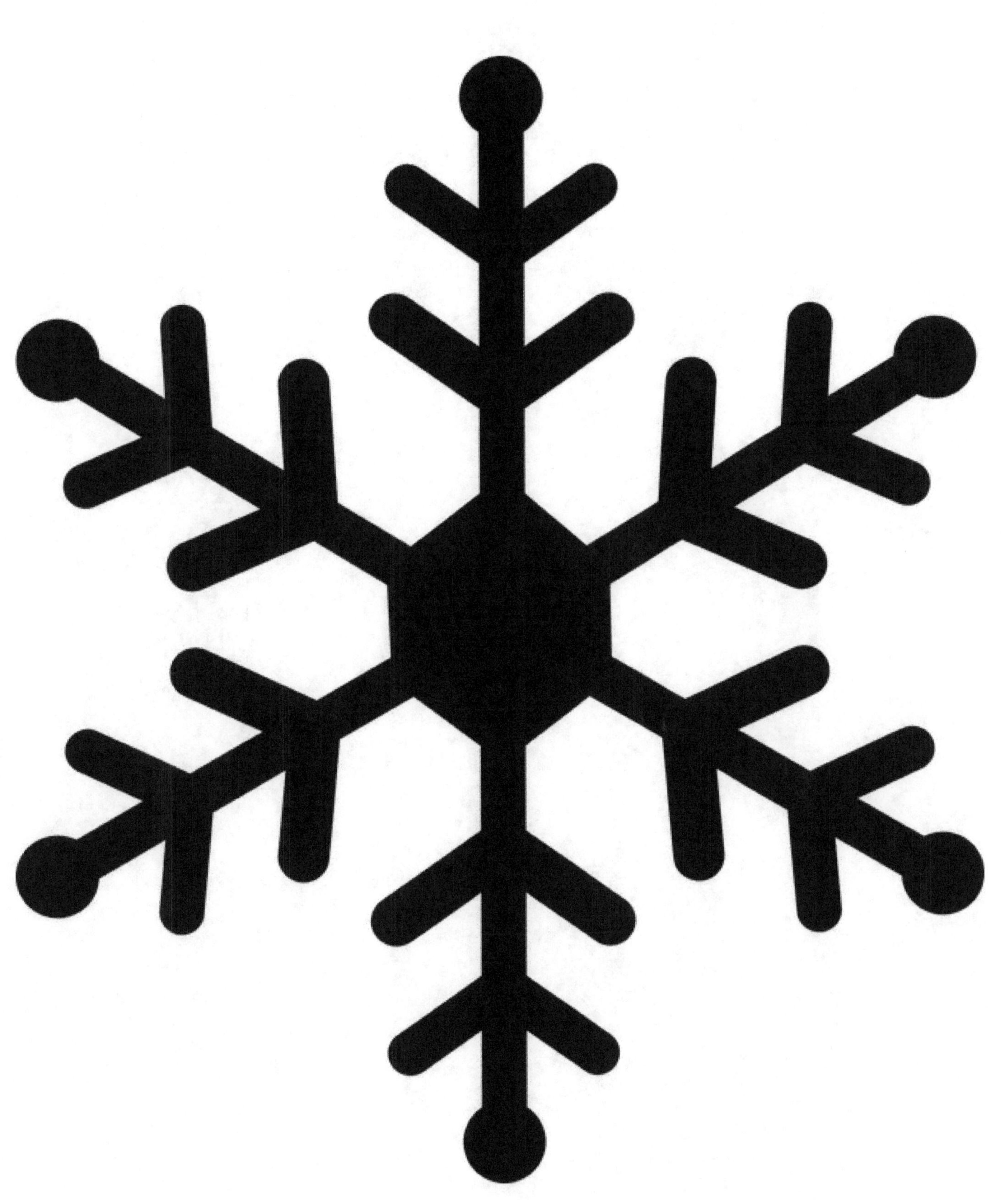

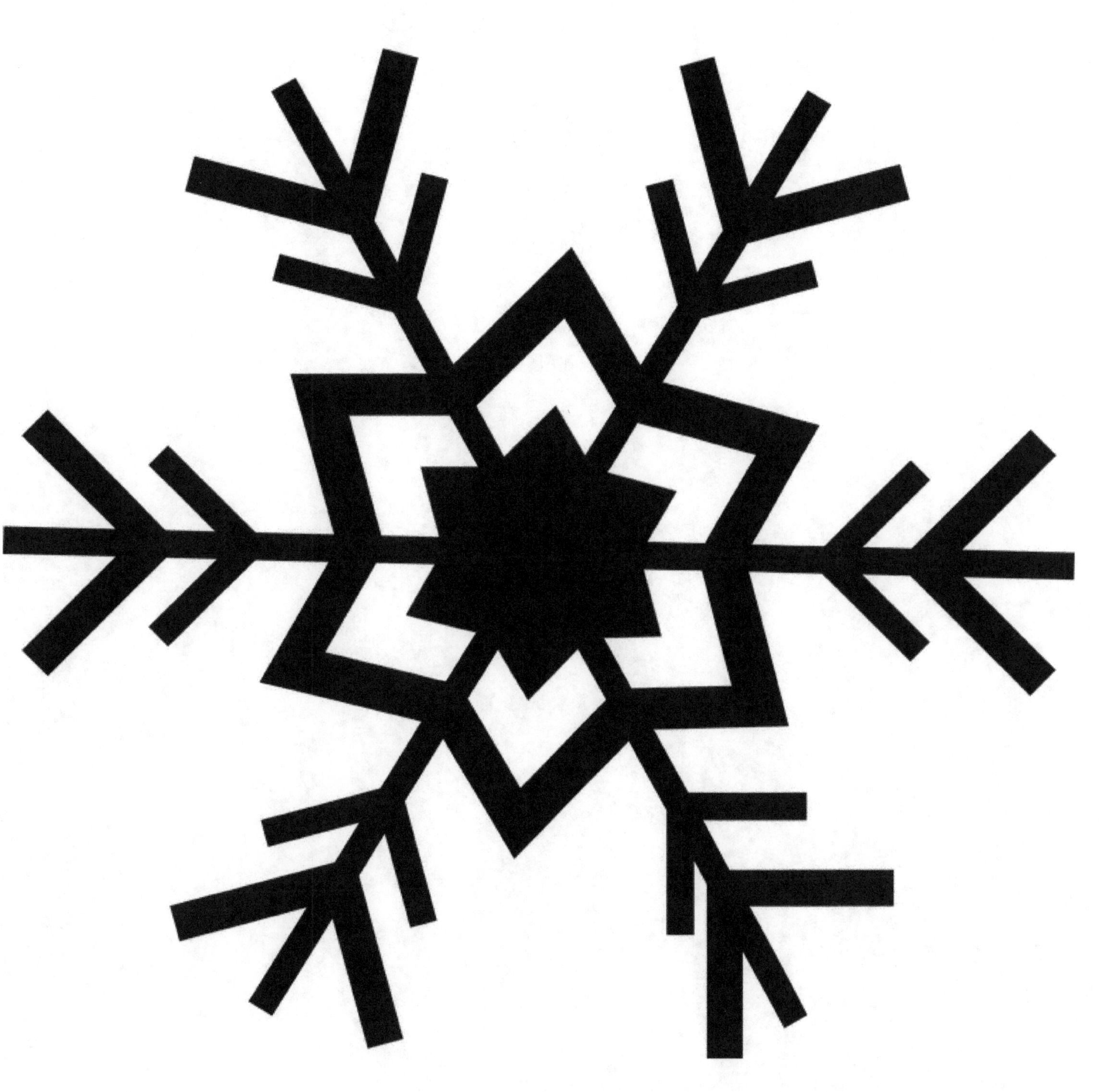

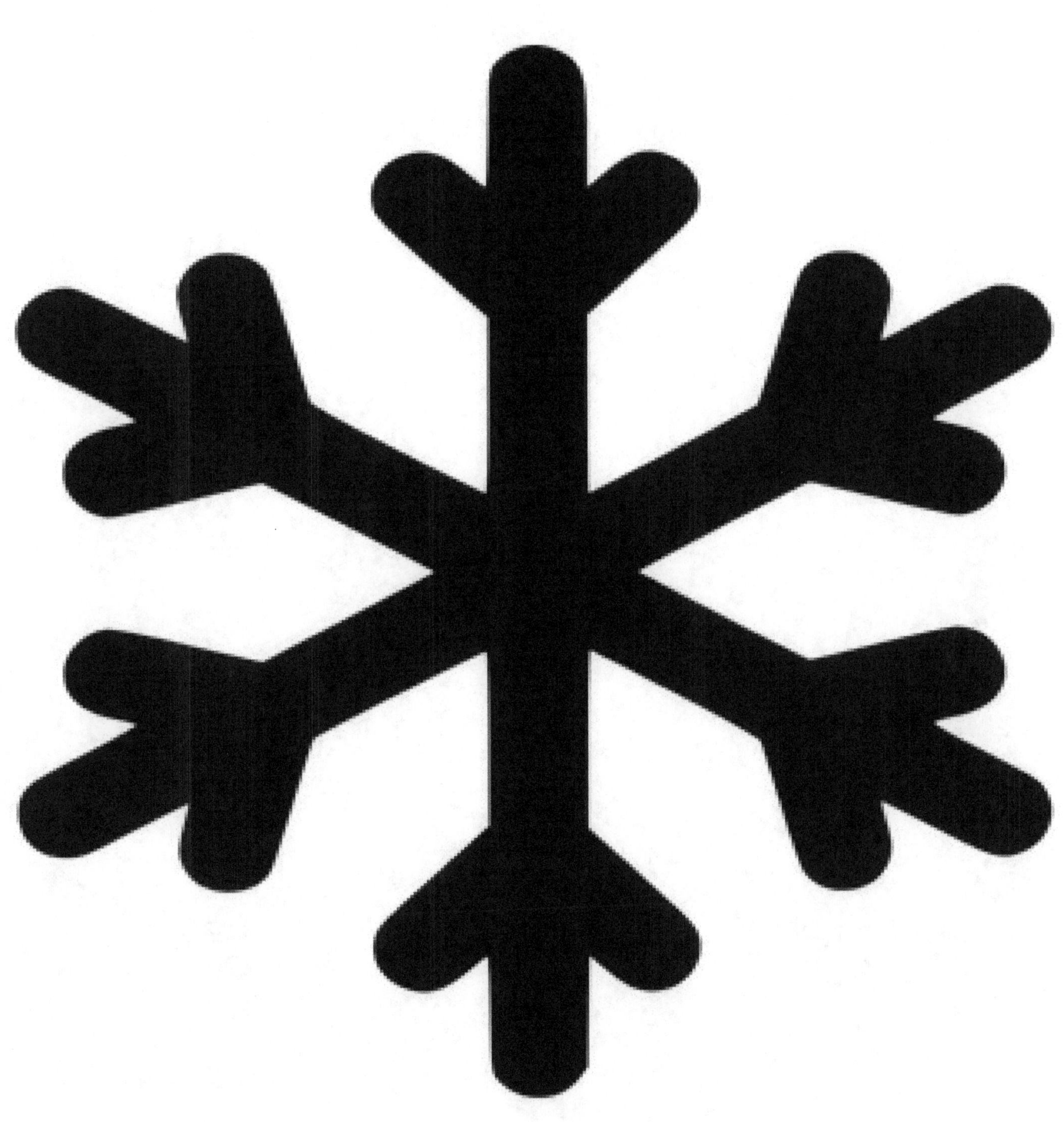

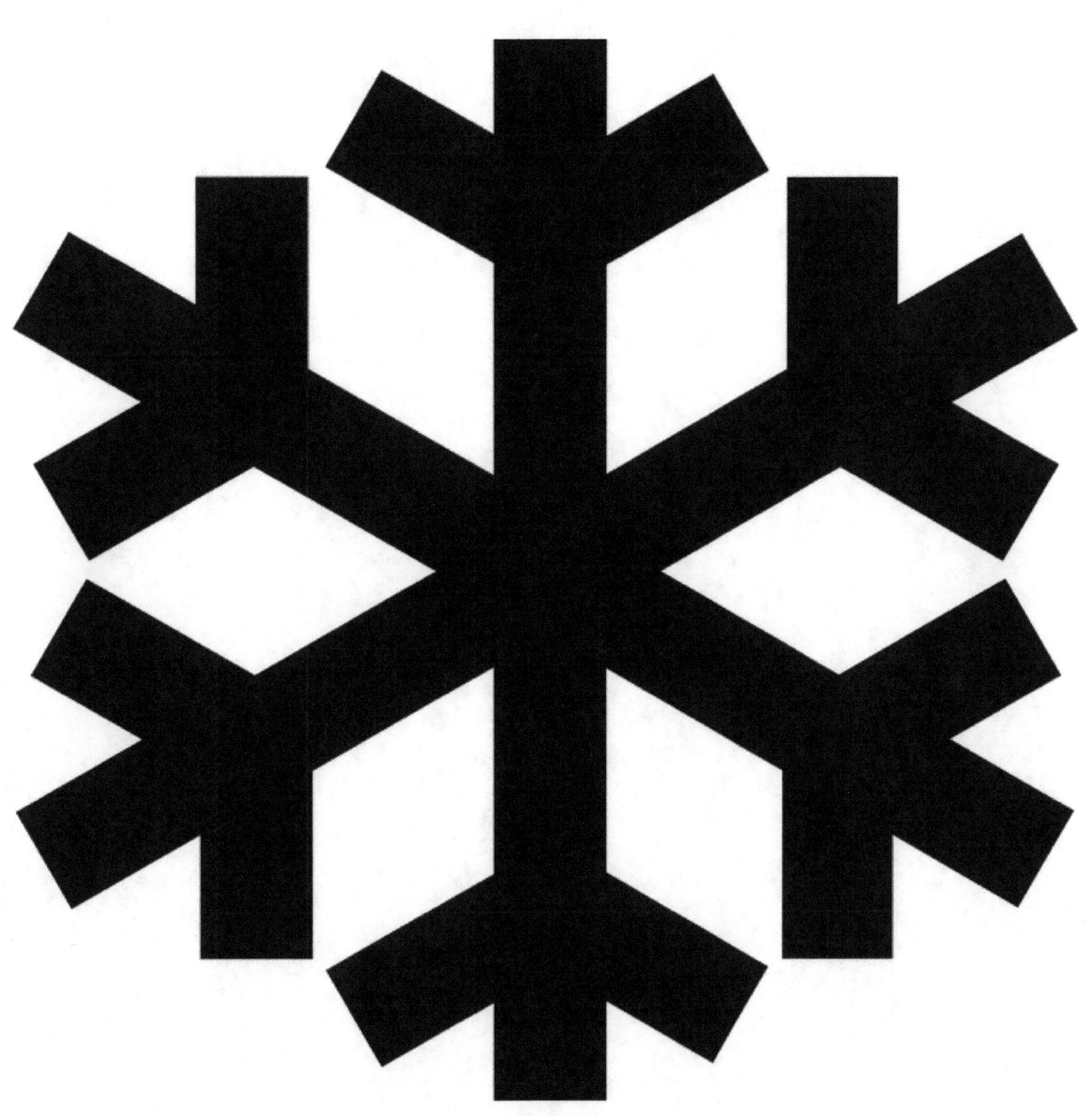

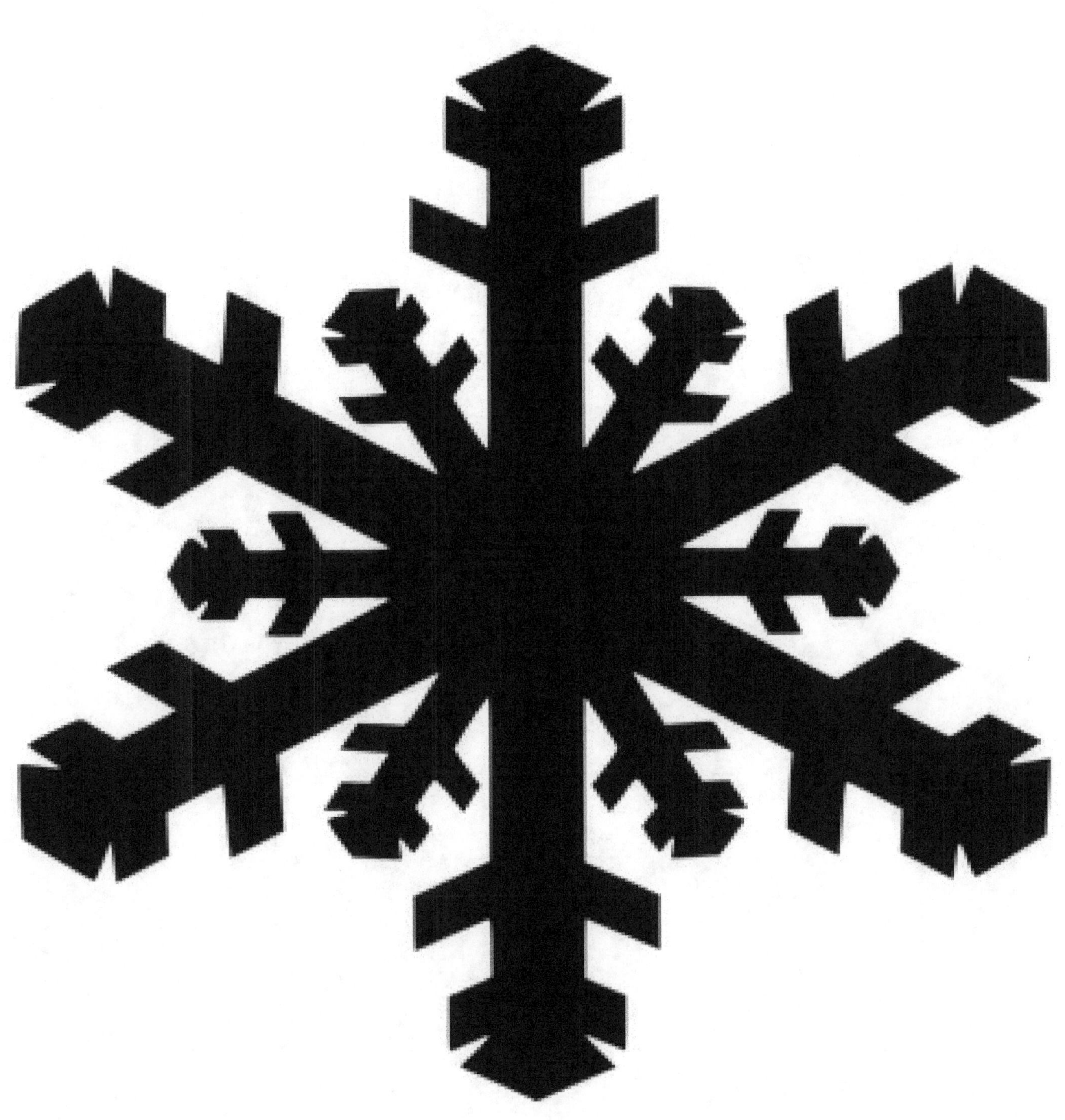

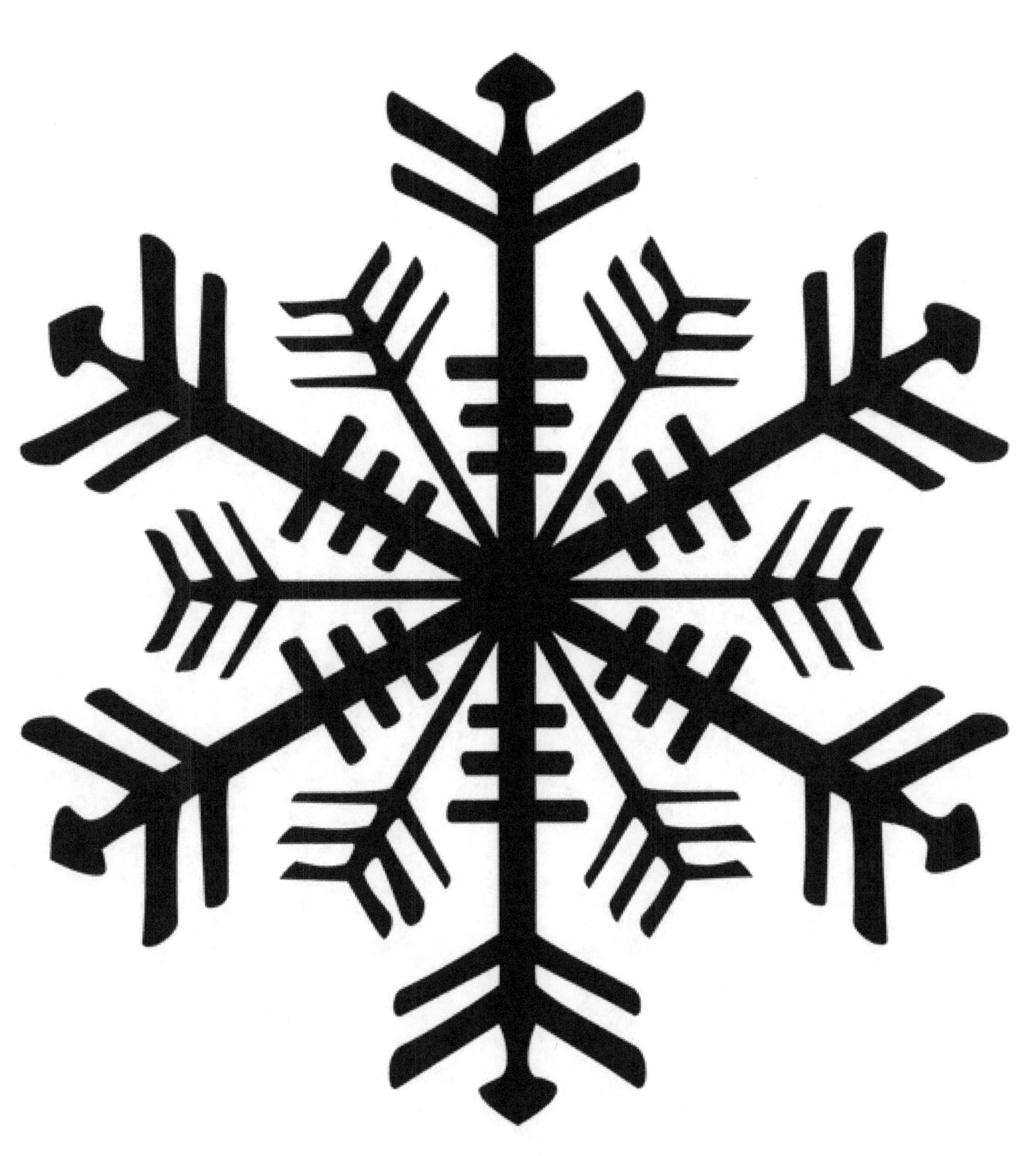

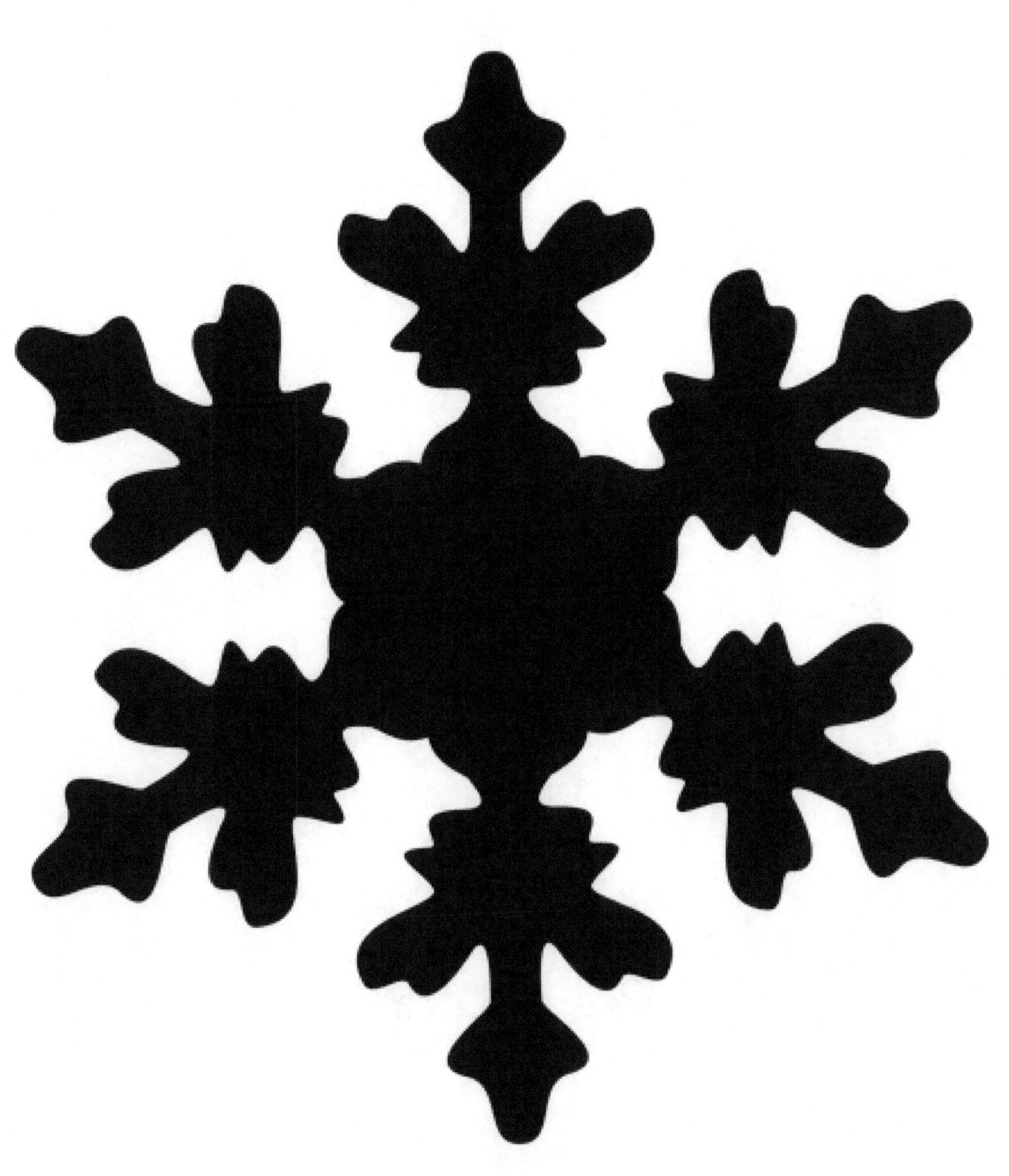

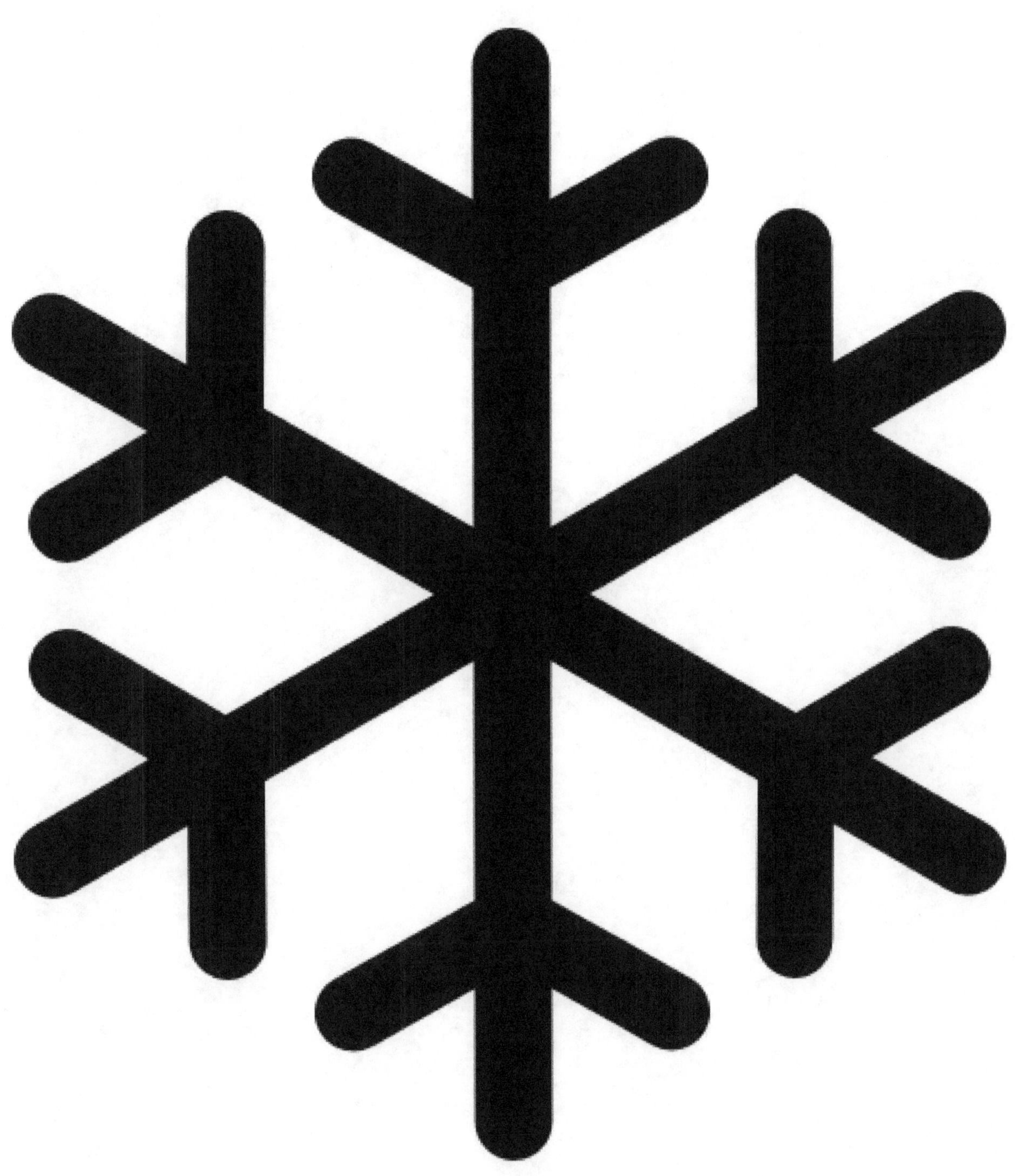